30-DAY DEVOTIONAL

YOU WIN

Biblical principles to recognizing the magnificent power within.

AMY WIENANDS

You Win 30-Day Devotional: Biblical Principles to Recognizing the Magnificent Power Within
Copyright © 2025 Amy Wienands
Published by You Are More Publishing

All rights reserved. No part of this publication can be reproduced, stored in a retrievable system, or transmitted in any form or by any means electronic, mechanical, photocopying, recording, or otherwise, except by the inclusion of brief quotations in a printed review, without prior written permission from the Publisher.

Scripture quotations taken from the Amplified® Bible (AMP), Copyright © 2015 by The Lockman Foundation. Used by permission. Lockman.org.

Scripture quotations from the COMMON ENGLISH BIBLE (CEB) © Copyright 2011. COMMON ENGLISH BIBLE. All rights reserved. Used by permission. (www.CommonEnglishBible.com).

Scripture quotations are from the ESV® Bible (The Holy Bible, English Standard Version®), © 2001 by Crossway, a publishing ministry of Good News Publishers. Used by permission. All rights reserved. The ESV text may not be quoted in any publication made available to the public by a Creative Commons license. The ESV may not be translated in whole or in part into any other language."

Scriptures marked KJV are taken from the KING JAMES VERSION (KJV): KING JAMES VERSION, public domain.

Scripture quotations marked MSG are taken from THE MESSAGE, copyright © 1993, 2002, 2018 by Eugene H. Peterson. Used by permission of NavPress. All rights reserved. Represented by Tyndale House Publishers, Inc.

Scripture quotations marked (NIV) are taken from the Holy Bible, New International Version®, NIV®. Copyright © 1973, 1978, 1984, 2011 by Biblica, Inc.™ Used by permission of Zondervan. All rights reserved worldwide. www.zondervan.com The "NIV" and "New International Version" are trademarks registered in the United States Patent and Trademark Office by Biblica, Inc.™

Scriptures marked NKJV are taken from the NEW KING JAMES VERSION (NKJV): Scripture taken from the NEW KING JAMES VERSION®. Copyright© 1982 by Thomas Nelson, Inc. Used by permission.

Scripture quotations marked (NLT) are taken from the Holy Bible, New Living Translation, copyright ©1996, 2004, 2015 by Tyndale House Foundation. Used by permission of Tyndale House Publishers, Carol Stream, Illinois 60188. All rights reserved.

Paperback ISBN: 979-8-9896028-1-0
Hardback ISBN: 979-8-9896028-3-4

TABLE OF CONTENTS

Introduction 1
Day 1: Oneness 5
Day 2: The God of Increase 9
Day 3: The Speaking Life 11
Day 4: The Benefit Package 15
Day 5: The Power of Your Secret Council 17
Day 6: The God Who Opens Doors 21
Day 7: Don't Give Up—Praise Through 25
Day 8: All Our Battles Are Winnable 29
Day 9: Favor Factor 33
Day 10: Guard Your Heart 37
Day 11: Faith Is an Action Word 41
Day 12: The Game-Changing Law of Sowing and Reaping 45
Day 13: Your Daily Habits Are Your Future 47
Day 14: The Righteous Come Out of Trouble 51
Day 15: Guard Your Mouth 55
Day 16: The Weapon of Praise 57
Day 17: Following God Wholeheartedly 61
Day 18: Victory Is in My Step! 65
Day 19: The Power of Your Choice 67
Day 20: The Purpose of Pain 71
Day 21: You Serve a Winning God 75
Day 22: God Is a Restorer 79
Day 23: Sing to Yourself 83
Day 24: Spending Time in the Word 87
Day 25: The Prision of Inconsistency 91
Day 26: Grace, Grace 95
Day 27: The Get-Back-Up Life 97
Day 28: Reviving Dry Bones 101
Day 29: Give Thanks Always 105
Day 30: Pray Bold Prayers 109
Conclusion 113

INTRODUCTION

The winning life is not necessarily associated with Christians—in fact, very much the opposite. Today, the world sees the church as a place for those who are defeated, who struggle through life, and who are broke. Many think Christianity is a crutch for weak people.

The truth is the exact opposite! Jesus came to equip you to do the supernatural and to reign over and possess all things. This is how you win! I want to help you get to know God on a deeply profound level as He transforms your thoughts and expectations with a deep understanding of Romans 8:28: that ALL things are working for your good.

A few years ago, I was out walking and praying when Ruth Ann Polston's name kept coming to my mind. For many, the name Ruth Ann Polston may not be widely known, but back in her day, she and her husband, Don H. Polston, blazed a remarkable trail for the gospel. Their ministry wasn't confined to my community. It reached far and wide. Ruth Ann and Pastor Don ministered at places like Robert Schuller's Crystal Cathedral and Dr. Paul Yonggi Cho's Prayer Mountain, touching lives across all 50 states and around the globe.

The Polstons also launched a TV ministry and books under the banner of The Life That Wins Ministries, led one of the largest Wesleyan churches in the nation, and counted legends like Norman Grubb and Charles "Tremendous" Jones among their friends.

Our family attended the Polston's church when I was a young girl. So, when Ruth Ann came to my mind that day, I couldn't ignore it. I knew she was in her 90s, and I wasn't sure how she would be physically or mentally. So, I decided to search YouTube to see if I could find anything recent about her. To my delight, I found a video recorded just months earlier of her playing the piano! That was all the confirmation I needed to reach out.

I called Ruth Ann and told her I wanted to meet her. She was so kind and invited me to attend her weekly Bible study. But I felt a stirring in my spirit that this wasn't just about a Bible study. I said to her, "Ruth Ann, I'd like to meet with you one-on-one. I feel like you have something I need." She agreed, and at 92 years young, she began to mentor me, pouring every truth God had given her into my life.

From the very first meeting, I knew this was a divine connection. Ruth Ann had spent countless hours in the presence of God, and I sensed this relationship was not just for me but for those I would one day impart her teachings to. What I didn't know was that Ruth Ann had been asking God to make the rest of her years count. She had prayed for someone to pour her life's work into.

Our prayers intersected.

For two and a half years, we met every Wednesday. Our time together quickly expanded to multiple times a week as I found her apartment to be a place of peace and refreshing.

We worshiped around the piano, and she poured out lessons she had prepared just for me. Every conversation was rich with truth, precepts, and revelations wrapped in the ever-unfolding beauty of Jesus. Ruth Ann truly taught me with God on my side I can't lose. And that God has called us to win in life—in every area!

Ruth Ann and I have become quite close. I treasure our time together, and I shift my schedule around because my time with Ruth Ann is sacred. There are relationships that God chooses for you—ones you don't expect but that leave an eternal impact on your soul. Take time to appreciate and honor those God has placed in your life—they are treasures beyond measure.

In 2024, Ruth Ann turned 96. Some things have changed over the past few months. Her handwriting has become difficult to read, and our conversations are mostly about heaven—who she will meet first and what it will be like. She is excited to go. I sense my time on earth with her is fading, and our relationship is changing. We still sit together, enjoying one another's presence, but now, I read to her.

This 30-day journal is a collection of principles, revelations, and truths Ruth Ann has poured into me. My prayer is that these words will revolutionize your life as you discover the power of living a victorious, winning life through the quickened Word of God.

When we seek first the kingdom of God, all these things (wholeness, health, money, wealth, security, peace) shall be added unto you. John 10:10 says that Jesus came that we might have life and have it more abundantly. Not just in heaven… but here on this earth. The Victorious One lives on the inside of you—and He will always lead you in victory.

Take a 30-day journey to discover the victorious life that Jesus came to give you!

YOU WIN!

DAY 1

ONENESS

But he that is joined unto the Lord is one spirit.
                                —1 Corinthians 6:17, KJV

Let's talk about the life-changing principle of oneness. You and God are one spirit—NOT two! Another verse that ties so closely to 1 Corinthians 6:17 is 1 John 4:17, "... as he is, so *are we* in this world" (KJV, emphasis mine).

The same God who created the heavens and the earth lives and dwells inside of you. Resurrection power lives inside of you! The Victorious One lives inside of you!

[To God's people] God has chosen to make known among the Gentiles the glorious riches of this mystery, which is Christ in you, the hope of glory.
                                —Colossians 1:27, NIV, emphasis mine

In order for Him to accomplish things on this earth, God set up His kingdom to partner with man. Ruth Ann always said, "God could accomplish anything by Himself, but has chosen man (as crazy and humbling as it may be), to be the counterpart." God is our collaborator. He comes alongside us to add His "super" to our "natural."

Ruth Ann told me of a time when she was playing and singing at an event, and she literally blew it.

My singing was awful, and I walked away not knowing if I would ever sing in front of people again. The next time I was asked, I pondered my ability to sing, and I heard the Lord say to me that it wasn't me who would be singing—it was Him! All the pressure went away. I agreed to the engagement, and when I started to perform, I closed my eyes and belted the song out. When I opened my eyes, the entire audience was standing and praising! That great mystery of Christ in me—the hope of glory—became manifest to me that day.

As I began to understand that God and I were truly partners in all things, and that I had the divine counsel of the victorious, all-knowing One who possesses all wisdom living inside me, I started to release Him to be the CEO of my company, as well as the mom, wife, friend, and leader I was called to be. God put His supernatural on my natural, and I realized that the line between where He ended and I began could no longer be detected.

That's the goal, isn't it?

We are an expression of Him; all that He is, we are (by the Spirit). All that He is not, we are not! As we lean into the person of Jesus, knowing that we are co-laborers with Him to bring about the will of God on this earth in all things, we rest, we trust, and we follow His Spirit.

Before you walk into a meeting, a presentation, or anything else, consider stopping to acknowledge God. I often say something like, "Let's go, God. I release You to be all things that I am not. I release You to be my wisdom, to lead, guide, and direct every word and step. Thank You for giving me supernatural empowerment to succeed in all things."

This is how in all things—you win!

YOU WIN: Write about a time you felt inadequate. How could inviting God's power to partner with you have changed the outcome?

DAY 2

THE GOD OF INCREASE

> *May the Lord give you increase more and more, You and your children. May you be blessed by the LORD, who made heaven and earth. The heaven, even the heavens, are the LORD'S; but the earth He has given to the children of men.*
> —Psalm 115:14-16, NKJV

> *Then God blessed them, and God said to them, "Be fruitful and multiply; fill the earth and subdue it; have dominion over the fish of the sea, over the birds of the air, and over every living thing that moves on the earth."*
> —Genesis 1:28, NKJV

The blessings given in the above verses are an empowerment to prosper. It's enabling us to succeed and increase. When you understand that heaven backs your growth and your accomplishments, it gives you the confidence to step out as God leads.

So often, we label defeat and a lack of success as God's will, but God is a God of increase who came to empower us to possess all things. When I pray, I often declare that everything I touch prospers and succeeds—that it will expand and increase supernaturally.

As Ruth Ann taught me, "Believe it, receive it, and act on it."

His divine power has given us everything we need for a godly life through our knowledge of him who called us by his own glory and goodness.

—2 Peter 1:3, NIV

God cares about every aspect of our lives—our families, our food, our bank accounts, and our calling. He holds it all together as if in a container with our name on it, sustaining it with His mighty power.

What do you need to speak a blessing over? Your business? Your finances? Your marriage? Your children? A dream? Remember that God is backing you and delights in seeing you increase and expand. Take heart and step forward with boldness in your life today!

As Ruth Ann often reminded me, "Dream big! Think big!" When you keep God first in your life, you cannot lose. He loves to partner with you and add good success to all you do. You represent Him and God loves to show off strong in your life.

This is how in all things—you win!

YOU WIN: What area of your life do you need to speak a blessing over today? Write a declaration of increase, inviting God to partner with you for success, growth, and expansion.

_____

_____

_____

_____

_____

DAY 3

THE SPEAKING LIFE

> *And God said, "Let there be light," and there was light.*
> —Genesis 1:3, NIV

God said let there be and there was. The Holy Spirit lives within us and has given us that same creative power. It's not solely our words that bring it to pass. Remember, it's His "super" adding to our "natural." This is why it's important to agree with and verbalize the things that God says about you and your life.

We don't need to create a new world, but we do play a role in shaping our own unique world. The same principles God used in creation have been made available to us.

Let's look at some Scripture to back up this principle.

> *You will also declare a thing, and it will be established for you; so light will shine on your ways.*
> —Job 22:28, NKJV

> *…I am watching to see that my word is fulfilled.*
> —Jeremiah 1:12, NIV

> *And the Word became flesh and dwelt among us….*
> —John 1:14, NKJV

God created with His Word; if He did it with His Word, we can too.

> But what does it say? "The word is near you, in your mouth and in your heart" (that is, the word of faith which we preach).
> —Romans 10:8, NKJV

As Genesis 1 reminds us, God said, let there be… and there was! He calls those things that are not as though they are (Romans 4:17).

I often find myself returning to the book of Joshua. In chapter ten, we see Joshua and his army fighting battles.

> Then Joshua spoke to the LORD in the day when the LORD delivered up the Amorites before the children of Israel, and he said in the sight of Israel: "Sun, stand still over Gibeon; and Moon, in the Valley of Aijalon," so the sun stood still, and the moon stopped, till the people had revenge upon their enemies. Is this not written in the Book of Jasher? So the sun stood still in the midst of heaven, and did not hasten to go down for about a whole day. And there has been no day like that, before it or after it, that the LORD heeded the voice of a man; for the LORD fought for Israel.
> —vv. 12-14, NKJV

This extraordinary moment demonstrates God's power and willingness to fight for His people. That's why there is so much power when we speak life. Remember, Proverbs 18:21 tells us, "Death and life are in the power of the tongue." God has given us authority to speak to our situations and demand that things turn in our favor.

> Thus says the LORD, the Holy One of Israel, and his Maker: "Ask Me of things to come concerning My sons; and concerning the work of My hands, you command Me."
> —Isaiah 45:11, NKJV

This challenges the thinking of many Christians—do you really mean I can command the hand of God? Yes, if it aligns with the Word of God, then you have the authority to do so. You can speak to sickness, lack, and limitation, and demand they release you or the person you're interceding for, based on the authority of God's Word. Find the promise in Scripture, stand on it, and then speak to that mountain with boldness.

Remember, as He is, so are you in this world. God always shows up where He is recognized. The world, our circumstances, and life itself constantly try to make us forget who we are in God and who He is in us. We are LITERALLY an extension of Him.

When you show up, God shows up! This is how in all things—you win!

YOU WIN: *Write a declaration for your life based on God's Word, speaking life, victory, and breakthrough.*

DAY 4

THE BENEFIT PACKAGE

> *Blessed be the Lord, Who daily loads us with benefits, the God of our salvation!*
>
> —Psalm 68:19, NKJV

The fact that the Lord said "daily" means we need provision and supply every single day—not monthly, not yearly, but daily.

Often, when I go for my morning walk, I thank God that His mercies are new every morning. I literally say, "Thank You for Your mercies, and I draw upon them for my life." When we begin to draw from divine supply and substance, all things become possible, and all things become changeable.

When we release Him to be what we are not, He becomes our patience, our wisdom, our help, our supply, and our peace. He is our "full benefits package." We can draw on these benefits when we recognize they are available to us. Most people go through life unaware that with God, there is a built-in system of supply and blessing.

God is a rewarder of those who diligently seek Him. He adds benefits to the lives of those who seek Him and do His work.

Here's some wisdom on the subject from Ruth Ann:

> *Supply belongs to need. Lack is an illusion. God's work done God's way will have God's supply. "Need" stands in the presence of the Father with its cup right side up and a smile on*

its face. "Lack" stands in the presence of the Father with its cup upside down and a frown on its face.

What benefit package do you need to draw on today?

> *If you stand on the ground of what Christ is in you, you will find that all that is true of Him is true of you: but, if you speak of what you are in your old self, you will find that all that is true of your old nature is true of you.*
>
> —Watchman Nee

Remember, you win!

YOU WIN: What part of God's "benefits package" do you need to draw on today—peace, wisdom, provision, or something else? Write a prayer of gratitude and ask Him to supply your need as you turn your cup upright in faith.

DAY 5

THE POWER OF YOUR SECRET COUNCIL

> *If any of you lacks wisdom, let him ask of God, who gives to all liberally and without reproach, and it will be given to him.*
> —James 1:5, NKJV

I've always called the Holy Spirit my "secret sauce" and my "unfair competitive advantage." One verse I've claimed and continue to stand on is:

> *The Lord GOD has given me the tongue of the learned, that I should know how to speak a word in season to him who is weary. He awakens me morning by morning; He awakens my ear to hear as the learned.*
> —Isaiah 50:4, NKJV

> *The Spirit of truth. The world cannot accept him, because it neither sees him nor knows him. But you know him, for he lives with you and will be in you.*
> —John 14:17, NIV

If it's wisdom you need—ASK!

> *If any of you lacks wisdom, let him ask of God, who gives to all liberally and without reproach, and it will be given to him. But let him ask in faith, with no doubting, for he who doubts is like a wave of the sea driven and tossed by the wind.*
> —James 1:5-6, NKJV

*The secret things belong to the L*ORD *our God, but those things which are revealed belong to us and to our children forever, that we may do all the words of this law.*
—Deuteronomy 29:29, NKJV

*I will bless the L*ORD *who has given me counsel; My heart also instructs me in the night seasons.*
—Psalm 16:7, NKJV

Asking God for wisdom doesn't have to be overcomplicated. It can be as simple as saying, "God, I need Your wisdom concerning (insert issue)." Then, be aware when a thought, an idea, or instruction comes to your mind regarding that situation. Sometimes, it comes immediately after I pray, but most often, it comes later while I'm doing other everyday tasks. That's how the Holy Spirit will talk to us. It doesn't have to be a "holy" moment. He is with us all the time.

In my life, I've learned that the more I listen to my spirit—whether you call it a gut feeling, intuition, or inner witness—the stronger it gets. I truly trust my spirit; it's my compass. I've come to deeply rely on the Counselor who lives inside me.

So often, things aren't as they appear. What looks one way to your flesh can feel completely different on the inside. Trust that inner voice! It will save you so much heartache and setback. There's power and protection in trusting your secret counsel.

YOU WIN: Think about an area in your life where you need clarity or direction. Write down a question to ask for wisdom, like, "What should I do about...?" Then reflect on how you can tune in to your inner compass (Holy Spirit) and stay open to ideas or insights that come to you.

DAY 6

THE GOD WHO OPENS DOORS

> *As thou goest step by step He will open up the way before you.*
> —Proverbs 4:12, paraphrased

Sometimes I find myself wanting things to happen so quickly—I'm tempted to kick the door open or force things to happen on my own. But I've learned that my focus should be on continuing to do the work and showing up as my best self.

As I keep moving forward, doing the next right thing, I am reminded of the Word:

> *The steps of a good man are ordered by the LORD, and He delights in his way.*
> —Psalm 37:23, NKJV

My steps are ordered—I declare that daily.

> *But the path of the just is like the shining sun, that shines ever brighter unto the perfect day.*
> —Proverbs 4:18, NKJV

My path is growing brighter every day!

> *As thou goest step by step, He'll open up the way before you.*
> —Proverbs 4:12, paraphrased

It's hard to trust sometimes that we're on the right path, especially when it feels like nothing is happening. You might have a big dream that seems like it will never come to pass or a health condition where answers and healing feel out of reach.

God doesn't operate on our timeline, but if we trust the process and commit our ways to Him, He will reorder circumstances and people for our good. He is an on-time God, always working—even behind the scenes.

The Scripture says that God opens doors that no man can close and closes doors that no man can open (Revelation 3:7). God is your door keeper. Other people can't keep you out of your purpose. Obstacles can't keep you from what God ordained for you.

This poem attributed to Arthur E. Ritchie beautifully captures this truth:

> *One step thou seest—then go forward boldly;*
> *One step is far enough for faith to see;*
> *Take that, and thy next duty shall be told thee,*
> *For step by step, thy Lord is leading thee.*

Trust and declare: "My steps are ordered by the Lord! As I go step by step, He opens up the way before me!"

Try it! Then, in all things—you win!

YOU WIN: Where in your life do you feel tempted to rush or force things to happen? Write about how you can trust the process and take the next step, believing your path is growing brighter every day.

DAY 7

DON'T GIVE UP—PRAISE THROUGH

But one thing I do: Forgetting what is behind and straining toward what is ahead, I press on toward the goal to win the prize for which God has called me heavenward in Christ Jesus.
—Philippians 3:13b-14, NIV

The following was written by Ruth Ann. I believe that it will encourage you.

Have you ever felt like giving up on prayer? Not just nice nighttime prayer. It's the time element of prayer delay when we don't see anything happening that tempts us to let up.

Continual asking will wear you out if you don't see some action. Have you thought about the possibility that the perpetual asking may be a form of unbelief?

"God is not a man, that He should lie…. hath He spoken and shall he not make it good?"
—Number 23:19, KJV

The Scriptures are full of how the "effectual fervent prayer of a righteous man availeth much" (James 5:16, KJV).

God wants us. It may be hard to believe, but He does. God is love and never will be anything else. We have His love letter to us in His Word. When the Word of God comes alive in us, we will begin to live it and our asking will turn to "thanking" and "praising." "Thanks" is the other side of asking.

Thank God that He's having His way in (write in your own circumstance).

Praise Him that things "work together for good to them that love God, to them who are the called according to his purpose" (Romans 8:28, KJV).

Perhaps God desires a deeper fellowship with you—one where prayer becomes a way of life. Instead of simply asking for things and waiting for the results, He invites you to praise Him in faith, even before the answers come.

King Jehoshaphat and his people were threatened by a country stronger than their own (2 Chronicles 20). Their first reflex was to be alarmed... which is our first reaction. We see with earthly eyes, not heaven's view. Jehoshaphat proclaimed a fast and prayer time for himself and his people. He put his head between his knees and sought the Lord. His whole viewpoint was altered.

He prepared his people by getting them in formation, but then told them they would not have to fight in that battle. Then he put singers in the front rank. Have you thought about singing your way through conflicting circumstances?

King Jehoshaphat knew Judah did not have the strength to stop the battle against Moab and Amon.

He just kept telling God how great a deliverer He was. He didn't know himself what to do, but if his eyes were on his delivering God then he was able to encourage his people. "The battle is not yours, but God's" (v. 15, KJV). He even told them to stand still and see the salvation of the Lord. Fear not!

And when they began to sing and shout, the attackers began to fight each other and in a short time their dead bodies littered the battle ground (vv. 22-24, NIV). Not one escaped. Note how Israel praised and shouted before the battle, not after. Turn your asking into praise. Immerse yourself in His Word and allow God to bring you to agreement with Him. You are no exception because He is no respecter of persons (Acts 10:34). He wants to win through you.

YOU WIN: What is something you've been praying for that feels delayed or unanswered? Write about how you can shift from asking to praising, trusting that God is already at work in your situation.

DAY 8

ALL OUR BATTLES ARE WINNABLE

Then all this assembly shall know that the Lord does not save with sword and spear; for the battle is the Lord's, and He will give you into our hands.
—1 Samuel 17:47, NKJV

Ruth Ann shared the following. Remember, you are already victorious!

In Joshua 5, our friend Joshua had brought the children over many desert miles. God, their Commander in Chief, had just parted the Jordan River while 2.5 million marched across on dry land. For three days of preparation, they camped just outside the forbidding walls of Jericho, the last city before Canaan, their promised land.

They must conquer Jericho, but how? While Israel slept, Joshua (wide awake) walked, waited, and listened. The God who took them out would take them "in."

"He is faithful that promised" (Hebrews 10:23. KJV).

Suddenly a man with a drawn sword appears before Joshua. Taken back, Joshua asks, "Are you for us or against us?"

"Neither," the man replied. "I am Captain of the Lord's host, who will fight the invisible armies of wicked spirits which have ruled Jericho with vice, witchcraft and many other wicked devices. Those armies will fight against our armies to maintain their status in Jericho and keep you from the land God promised you forever."

Of course, Joshua was eager to know what Israel's part was in the battle. The answer was so simple—it was profound. Walk!

Joshua would need chosen walkers who knew how to keep rank, even if what they were asked to do made no common sense. Sometimes the life of faith doesn't make sense.

All the armed men would be the first in rank.

Following would be the priests blowing the shofars (a trumpet blast).

Next came the ark carried on the priests' shoulders. Inside the ark were the ten commandments received by Moses on Mt. Sinai, Aaron's rod that budded, and a sample of manna which Israel ate as they traveled from Egypt.

More guards followed the ark.

On the last day, as the walkers circled Jericho, they shouted loudly, and the walls fell flat.

The unseen armies of God above and Israel's faith walk below had won. Israel sprang over the fallen walls and not a man of Jericho was left standing.

We've all had our hindering Jerichos that tried to keep us from our promised possession.

The captain of our salvation will not let us lose. God has invested His life in us. There has not one Word failed of all His promise (Joshua 21:45). What He has promised He is able also to perform (Romans 4:21).

Heaven will be full of stories of believers' victories who will share that all their battles were winnable.

What are some of your victories? Take a moment to thank God for the battles that He's already brought you through, and declare that any battle you are facing now—you win!

YOU WIN: What "Jerichos" in your life has God already helped you conquer? Write about those victories, thank Him for His faithfulness, and declare that the battles you're facing now will also end in victory!

DAY 9

FAVOR FACTOR

> *For You, O L*ORD*, bless the righteous man [the one who is in right standing with You]; You surround him with favor as with a shield.*
> —Psalm 5:12, AMP

Favor is a force that causes people to go out of their way to be good to you, granting you access and promotion. It can open doors that, in the natural, you might not be the "most qualified" for.

Graham Cooke wrote in his *Brilliant Perspectives* blog:

Favor is a lifestyle of ever-increasing, ever-expanding preference that upgrades our relationship with the Godhead and our status in the Kingdom. The development of favor goes hand-in-hand with learning the art of walking out and working in the truth of who Christ is for us and who we have permission to become in Him. Favor is best received as part of a joyful process that enables us to contend against our own negativity, and overcome every circumstance of life because we have found favor in the eyes of God!"[1]

The Word confirms this:

> *And so find favor and high esteem In the sight of God and man.*
> —Proverbs 3:4, NKJV

---

[1] *https://brilliantperspectives.com/training-life-favor*

And Jesus increased in wisdom and stature, and in favor with God and men.

—Luke 2:52, NKJV

Remember, "As He is, so are we in this world" (1 John 4:17, NKJV). Speak favor over your life—you can cooperate with it and even increase in it. It's often said, "One day of favor is worth more than a lifetime of effort."

Ruth Ann reminds us: "Jesus has placed me right by His side to win over the kingdom of darkness above the devil and sin." When God calls us, He equips us, but He also expects us to think big. He says to ask largely. Ruth Ann also says, "Jesus said to pray in His Name. He said for me to command Him. His prayers and mine are the same."

Terri Savelle Foy shared that God once told her, "Ask Me for something that makes Me look like God." This challenges us to ask boldly. Too often, our prayers focus on needs rather than big, God-sized dreams.

God's dream for us requires His supernatural favor to accomplish. You have the ability to increase in favor, but first, you need to know that you have supernatural access to it. His favor is a shield around you.

May the favor of the Lord our God rest on us; establish the work of our hands for us.

—Psalm 90:17, NIV

6 STEPS TO INCREASING FAVOR

1. Seek first the kingdom of God, and all these things shall be added to you.

   - Put God first in your mornings.
   - Put God first in your week.
   - Put God first in your marriage.

- Put God first in your finances.

2. When you feel led to do something, do it. You can't move past your last act of disobedience.
3. Keep your heart clean.
4. Be a giver—a tither.
5. Speak favor.
6. Expect favor.

As you go about your day, declare favor over your life. Before appointments, discussions, or opportunities, speak it out loud: "I'm favored. I increase in favor with both God and man daily."

God wants you to win. Our lives should be ever-increasing and ever-abounding. Speak favor, expect favor, cooperate with the Spirit of God, and respond when He leads you—and watch Him swing big doors open for you!

Remember... you win!

YOU WIN: Where do you need to see God's favor at work in your life right now? Write a declaration of favor, boldly asking God to open doors, grant access, and bring supernatural promotion in that area. Then, list one way you can cooperate with His leading today.

_____

_____

_____

DAY 10

GUARD YOUR HEART

Above all else, guard your heart, for everything you do flows from it.
—Proverbs 4:23, NIV

God connects your soul to your health and wealth: "Beloved, I wish above all all things that thou mayest prosper and be in health, even as your soul prospereth" (3 John 2, KJV).

As your soul—your mind, body, and spirit—becomes healthy and whole, your external world begins to reflect that inner transformation, like a well-watered garden. But soul and heart work is a daily responsibility. You must guard against offense, bitterness, jealousy, discouragement, and anything else that seeks to snare you.

When you get snared by offense or lack, everything you see is filtered through that lens, and that lens perpetuates more lack and offense. Why? Because you always find what you're looking for. Think about that. Could it be that the sameness in your relationships, business, and even your walk with God comes down to the lens you're looking through?

Thoughts are powerful, and emotions can be even more so. Every situation we encounter is filtered through those lenses. When you feel rejected, hurt, or "not enough," you start to see everything through that lens. And it doesn't stop there—it actually produces situations and conversations that confirm those feelings and thoughts.

We are incredibly powerful—scary-cool powerful. I often say, "Our world looks exactly like how we think."

I've learned to keep a short account when it comes to my heart. Every day, I evaluate if I'm carrying offense or hurt toward anyone. If I am, I speak it out loud: "I release the hurt and offense. I release the energy of it from my body, my mind, and my emotions. I wash myself and the situation in the blood of Jesus." Then I ask the Holy Spirit to be my ability to forgive and move forward. Sometimes, depending on the closeness of the person, I have to do this multiple times—but I take it seriously.

Why? Because so many things I desire are connected to having my heart and mind in the right place. The Bible says:

> *A generous man [is a source of blessing and] shall be prosperous and enriched, and he who waters will himself be watered [reaping the generosity he has sown].*
>
> —Proverbs 11:25, AMP

Generosity is a heart issue. Are you generous in your attitudes and thoughts towards others? Do you wish them well and cheer them on without envy, jealousy, bitterness, or resentment?

Your heart decides, and your mind justifies. Guard what you allow to enter your mind and heart. Become the master of your inner world, and you'll see God bring promotion and abundant provision into your life.

YOU WIN: What thoughts or feelings might be shaping the lens you're viewing life through right now? Write about any hurt, offense, or negativity you need to release, and ask God to help you see yourself and others as He does… with generosity and love.

DAY 11

FAITH IS AN ACTION WORD

> *In the same way, faith by itself, if it is not accompanied by action, is dead. But someone will say, "You have faith; I have deeds." Show me your faith without deeds. and I will show you my faith by my deeds.*
>
> —James 2:17-18, NIV

Faith without action is not faith. Faith requires us to act, to take a step of faith. If we just sit and think without reaching or acting, God has nothing to work with. Faith is literally in your mouth.

To avoid letting thoughts run you ragged and drag your emotions down, you must become a third-party observer of yourself. Pay attention to the direction of your thought life, and then intentionally shift your thoughts. Our lives are a reflection of our thoughts, which produce feelings. Those feelings often shut us down and stop us in our tracks.

If you want to succeed in life, you have to tell your feelings to take a back seat. Life is an action-based economy—you will act your way into feeling differently and possessing your dreams. Faith is an action step, and without works, it's dead. Faith is an action word!

> *But without faith it is impossible to please Him, for he who comes to God must believe that He is, and that He is a rewarder of those who diligently seek Him.*
>
> —Hebrews 11:6, NKJV

In my own life, my real estate career has been my "school of faith." Building my company has taught me to use all my faith tools, and time and time again, God has revealed keys to create success. Faith is not just a belief—it's an act of trust that moves you into action, partnering with God to bring His promises to pass.

The first key is to **ACT**.

You have to take the step. I can stand and declare all day long that I'm the top agent in the state of Iowa or that our company has the best listings, all the high-end properties, or whatever else—but unless I'm actually out there making phone calls, meeting with people, and hosting open houses, it will never happen!

I can't just sit in my house, thinking that one day it's all just going to magically happen. That's a pipe dream! Yet so many of us live like that. We just sit there and hope. We hope our business will increase, our health will improve, or that things will somehow change. I call that basing your life on a wing and a prayer.

God always asks us to step out and act in faith.

Take action. Put your foot forward. Then He'll show you the next step. Put your foot forward again, and He'll reveal the next step. God is an action-oriented God; when we take action, we show that we trust Him. Our actions also give Him something to work with. If we never take an action step, we never plant a seed in the ground.

Faith is like a seed. A farmer plants the seed in good soil, waters it, and trusts it will grow—even when they can't see it yet. They *expect* it to produce! In the same way, you have to plant the seeds of faith in your life. You have to plant the seeds of action. Every single day, take an action step.

Take those steps with the mindset: "I trust You, God. I believe You, God."

So many things in my life have come down to just taking the next step—whether it was dating my husband, building a new building, starting a podcast, writing a book, speaking on stage, or taking the leap of faith to start my own company years ago.

Be focused. Be determined. Don't cater to the feelings you get from what your eyes see—or don't see. Don't let your progress or lack of it, what people say or don't say, stop you. Just keep taking the next step, and then the next step, and then the next step.

As you do, provision and people will come around you. They'll support you, encourage you, and even become part of your vision. God already has people assigned to assist you and be a part of all that He has prepared for you!

Remember: "As thou goest step by step, He'll open up the way before you."

What dream do you have that needs some action behind it? Take the step. Put action behind your dreams and visions, and watch God show off strong on your behalf.

YOU WIN: What dream or goal in your life needs action today? Write down one step you can take right now to move toward it. Ask God to guide your steps as you trust Him in the process.

_____

_____

_____

_____

DAY 12

THE GAME-CHANGING LAW OF SOWING AND REAPING

> *There is the one who [generously] scatters [abroad], and yet increases all the more; and there is the one who withholds what is justly due, but it results only in want and poverty. The generous man [is a source of blessing and] shall be prosperous and enriched, and he who waters will himself be watered [reaping the generosity he has sown].*
> —Proverbs 11:24-25, AMP

The Bible says, "He who has a generous eye will be blessed, For he gives of his bread to the poor" (Proverbs 22:9, NKJV).

Everything in your life is a seed. You are a seed sower and a harvest receiver. When you show kindness, you reap kindness. When you sow seeds of strife, competition, comparison, or jealousy, you'll reap those things too. Every word you speak is a seed into your future.

I live by this principle:

> *Do not withhold good from those to whom it is due, When it is in the power of your hand to do so.*
> —Proverbs 3:27, NKJV

If it's in the power of my hand to do good, then I do good. Keep doing the next right thing.

You can't sow jealous, bitter, lack-filled thoughts and expect abundance, plenty, and provision to show up in your life. I believe you play a vital role in determining the blessing of God in your life. You might go through a "season" of difficulty or lack, but it shouldn't become a lifetime of the same old, same old. If you don't like what you're seeing, it's time to change the seed you're sowing.

You have the ability to change your season, your relationships, your job, and your future—with the seed of your words.

When you choose to speak blessing, increase, and call those things that are not as though they are, you'll eat the fruit of that seed—and it will be good. Your tongue is a creative force for good or evil—so use it wisely!

That's how you win!

YOU WIN: What seeds are you sowing with your words and actions today? Reflect on how you can intentionally sow generosity, kindness, and blessing into your life and the lives of others. Write one specific way you'll start planting better seeds this week.

DAY 13

YOUR DAILY HABITS ARE YOUR FUTURE

Therefore, since we are surrounded by such a great cloud of witnesses, let us throw off everything that hinders and the sin that so easily entangles. And let us run with perseverance the race marked out for us, fixing our eyes on Jesus, the pioneer and perfecter of faith.

—Hebrews 12:1-2a, NIV

If I can observe your daily habits, I can easily predict your future. Your future is hidden in your daily routines.

"For who has despised the day of small things?" (Zechariah 4:10a, NKJV). Most beginnings don't look like much—they're typically small, boring action steps taken one day at a time. But if you can keep the vision before you, start with the end in mind, and hold it steady, those daily steps will eventually manifest into what others call "overnight success."

Those small, consistent, and often unnoticed actions begin to build on each other until the compound effect kicks in. Suddenly, you'll find that tiny, consistent steps swing big doors.

I've learned that approaching life with bite-sized micro-commitments makes winning easier, faster, and helps build a habit or pattern of success. For example:

If you're not a morning person but want to develop a strong morning routine, start by waking up just 15 minutes earlier. Master that first hurdle, and then increase it gradually.

- If you're working on your health, start with a short walk—one block, one mile—just get moving.

- Want to write a book? Start with one page a day.

- Launching a business? Take one small step forward each day.

When you stay consistent with these micro-commitments, you'll begin to walk with a different kind of confidence. That confidence will give you a high authenticity score—not just with yourself (the most important) but with others as well.

It's said that it takes 66 days to form a new habit. You won't see the weight drop after one workout, or your bank account grow after one week of saving, or your book finished after one page. But if you keep at it, one day you'll wake up and see the difference—on the scale, in your bank account, or in the finished work you've created.

Albert Einstein called compound interest the eighth wonder of the world. And while it has a massive impact on finances year over year, the principle works in every area of life.

As Martin Luther King Jr. famously said: "If you can't fly, then run; if you can't run, then walk; if you can't walk, then crawl. But by all means, keep moving!"

Movement is medicine. You must keep moving and taking steps.

If you don't quit—you will win!

YOU WIN: What is one small, consistent action you can take today toward a goal or dream? Write down your micro-commitment and how you'll stay consistent, trusting that even small steps will lead to big results over time.

DAY 14

THE RIGHTEOUS COME OUT OF TROUBLE

Do not rejoice over me, my enemy; When I fall, I will arise; When I sit in darkness, The Lord will be a light to me.
—Micah 7:8, NKJV

In God, whose word I praise, in the LORD, whose word I praise— in God I trust and am not afraid. What can man do to me?
—Psalm 56:10-11, NIV

Sometimes, I think people believe that when they accept Jesus, they'll have no problems. In reality, you'll likely face more challenges. The difference is that God equips you to move through, overcome, and triumph in your battles.

Here are your promises:

I sought the LORD, and He heard me, and delivered me from all my fears.
—Psalm 34:4, NKJV

The righteous will come through trouble.
—Proverbs 12:13, NKJV

The LORD is my light and my salvation; Whom shall I fear? The LORD is the strength of my life; Of whom shall I be afraid?
—Psalm 27:1, NKJV

I've walked through seasons of testing. I remember a time when I was served with lawsuit papers that completely blindsided me. I felt like my reputation and character were under attack, even though I knew I had done no wrong. I assumed it was an unfounded "money grab" that would be dismissed quickly, but to my dismay, it dragged on at every turn.

One Saturday morning, overwhelmed with stress, I cried out, "God, I need You to speak to me. What is going on?" I opened my Bible and landed on the story of Joseph. You know Joseph—the favorite son who shared his dream and made his brothers feel threatened, the one sold into slavery, falsely accused by Potiphar's wife, and thrown in prison.

Then I read:

> *But as for you, you meant evil against me; but God meant it for good, in order to bring it about as it is this day, to save many people alive.*
>
> —Genesis 50:20, NKJV

That verse took hold of me, and I quoted it multiple times a day.

I'd love to say the lawsuit ended quickly, but 18 months later, I found myself sitting in court, enduring jury selection. It was humiliating. I was told the jury wouldn't like me, that I stood to lose a lot, and that I needed to "dress down" and take on a completely different persona.

The trial dragged on for four days, and honestly, it wasn't going well. On the fifth day—a Friday—I was set to testify. I woke up nervous and anxious. But as I looked in the mirror while getting ready, I thought, *Wait a minute!* I reminded myself, *I've been going into people's homes for years. I've had great success. People like me!*

That shift in perspective changed everything. I walked into court with new confidence, and the difference was so noticeable that the plaintiff suddenly wanted to settle.

Against my attorney's advice, I refused to settle. They had put me through the wringer for a year and a half, and I felt a surge of confidence that God was with me. I needed to see this through.

When I took the stand and responded to several questions, I asked the judge for permission to speak directly to the jury. He agreed. Ten minutes into my statement, I saw the jury shift. They started nodding in agreement with me.

When I finished and returned to my seat, the plaintiff's attorney had no more questions. The judge reprimanded the plaintiff for trying to tarnish the reputation of "one of the greatest realtors in the Midwest" and dismissed the case entirely.

Not only did the lawsuit cost me nothing in attorney fees, but the seller's attorney was so appreciative of my testimony that he delivered a designer watch to my office the next day—he knew I loved watches!

God was faithful. Truly, what was meant to harm me, He turned for my good. And to top it off, I even gained a few new clients from the jury! Why? Because I refused to settle and trusted God. He is no respecter of persons.

If God will do it for me, He will do for you. Remember…you win!

YOU WIN: Think about a challenge or setback you're currently facing. How can you shift your perspective to trust that what's meant for harm, God can turn for your good? Write down a declaration of faith, believing that you will overcome and win.

DAY 15

GUARD YOUR MOUTH

> *Catch for us the foxes, the little foxes that ruin the vineyards, our vineyards that are in bloom.*
> —Song of Songs 2:15, NIV

Sometimes the words we speak are literally breathing death into our dreams and future.

> *Whoever desires to love life and see good days, let him keep his tongue from evil and his lips from speaking deceit.*
> —1 Peter 3:10, ESV

The Message version puts it this way, "Whoever wants to embrace life and see the day fill up with good, here's what you do: Say nothing evil or hurtful."

I remember the day this Scripture truly spoke to me. It was 2021, and I was walking through a health crisis. My focus was on life, health, and getting better—on overcoming and believing for a long, good life.

When I read this verse, a holy fear came over me. I wanted a long life and many good days, so I made a decision. Every time I was tempted to be critical or say anything negative about someone else, I stopped myself with this promise!

Even today, when I feel tempted to murmur or complain about someone, these words come to mind, and I'm reminded to "say not." I truly believe this is one of the strongest keys to experiencing the goodness of God in our lives—avoiding negative or evil talk about others.

Let's face it, I know it's so easy to do. How often have you wanted to spill the tea or share a juicy story about someone else? We're quick to call a friend or a group and let it all out. But when you're faced with a challenge and a word like this quickens your spirit, it becomes crucial to pay attention—especially if you want to embrace life and see good days.

Could this be a little "fox" in your life, nipping at the vine of your blessings?

Ask God to put a guard over your mouth when you're tempted to speak evil or negativity—whether about yourself or someone else. Remind yourself of this promise and declare out loud: "I will live long and see many, many good days, in Jesus' name!"

YOU WIN: Are there any "little foxes" in your words—negative or critical things you've been saying about yourself or others? Write a statement of life and blessings about those things instead, and ask God to help guard your words.

DAY 16

THE WEAPON OF PRAISE

> *The LORD is my strength and my shield; my heart trusts in him, and he helps me. My heart leaps for joy, and with my song I praise him.*
>
> —Psalm 28:7, NIV

Praise is the key to winning a battle. You don't just pray your way through a battle—you praise your way through it.

There are times when things are so difficult and emotional that praying feels almost impossible. Most of us have been there—when the battle rages on and isn't over in a minute. You've been dealing with the situation for what feels like forever. Your circumstances stare you in the face, mocking your faith. You're weary, and you're not sure if you can carry on or take the next step.

Praise is a powerful spiritual weapon against the enemy. "Resist the devil, and he will flee from you" (James 4:7, NIV).

Since God inhabits our praises, the enemy has no choice but to take flight. Darkness cannot stay in the presence of light.

So, praise your way through the storm.

What do I mean by praise? I mean speaking out of your mouth: "I praise You, God." Keep it simple. When thoughts of impossibility bombard your mind, just say it again: "I praise You, God." You can add more if you feel led, for example: "I praise You and worship You—there is no God like You. I magnify Your name."

At first, it might feel dry, like chewing on cotton balls—hard to speak out and with no emotion behind it. But that's okay. The key is speaking it out loud because it interrupts the cycle of negativity and destructive thoughts in your mind. Praise engages both your mind and your spirit.

It might feel like nothing is happening initially, but don't stop. The enemy wants you to believe it's not working. Keep praising, because praise is the place where you begin to hear God. Praise is faith in action, and faith has ears to hear.

Remember Paul and Silas in the jail cell? They prayed and informed God of their situation, but when they started to sing praises, something shifted. That's when they began to inform the enemy that they already had the victory—*through their praise.*

Praise is the release of faith.

If you're in a battle today, you can win by praising your way through. The Spirit of God will lead you into all truth and victory.

> *For the LORD your God is the one who goes with you to fight for you against your enemies to give you victory.*
> —Deuteronomy 20:4, NIV

> *But thanks be to God! He gives us the victory through our Lord Jesus Christ.*
> —1 Corinthians 15:57, NIV

> *I can do all things through Christ who strengthens me.*
> —Philippians 4:13, NKJV

YOU WIN: What battle are you facing right now? Write down a simple praise to God, declaring His power and faithfulness. Commit to speaking it out loud today, trusting that your praise is your path to victory.

FOLLOWING GOD WHOLEHEARTEDLY

Teach me your way, LORD, that I may rely on your faithfulness; give me an undivided heart, that I may fear your name.
—Psalm 86:11, NIV

Joshua is one of my favorite biblical giants. He followed Moses so closely, he honored him, he learned from him, he loved and respected Moses. One day, Moses, the trusted leader of Israel, went to heaven, and God said to Joshua:

Moses my servant is dead. Now then, you and all these people, get ready to cross the Jordan River into the land I am about to give to them.
—Joshua 1:2, NIV

Have I not commanded you? Be strong and courageous. Do not be afraid; do not be discouraged, for the LORD your God will be with you wherever you go.
—Joshua 1:9, NIV

Joshua was 45 years old when Moses sent him, Caleb, and the other 10 spies to explore the promised land. It was said of Caleb that he had a different spirit and followed God wholeheartedly.

So on that day Moses swore to me, "The land on which your feet have walked will be your inheritance and that of your children forever, because you have followed the LORD my God wholeheartedly."
—Joshua 14:9, NIV

At 85 years old, Caleb declared, "I am still as strong today as the day Moses sent me out; I'm just as vigorous to go out to battle now as I was then. Now give me this hill country that the LORD promised me that day" (Joshua 14:11-12, NIV).

Can you imagine having that kind of energy and enthusiasm at 85? Caleb's strength and zest for life were remarkable. What was the key? He *wholly followed the Lord.*

The word *wholly* means "all the time." It's not part-time devotion to God but full-time commitment. Caleb's unwavering faith brought extraordinary blessings. God gave him a different perspective. While others saw the land as filled with giants and impossible challenges, Caleb and Joshua saw opportunity and promise.

> *Then Caleb silenced the people before Moses and said, "We should go up and take possession of the land, for we can certainly do it."*
>
> —Numbers 13:30, NIV

In contrast, those who didn't follow God wholeheartedly saw themselves as grasshoppers in comparison to the giants, and they never entered the land. Their fear and disbelief caused millions of others to miss the promised land as well.

When you follow God wholly, it doesn't mean you won't face challenges—you absolutely will. That's why God commanded Joshua to be strong and have courage. Challenges will come, but God's promise is this:

> *The righteous person may have many troubles, but the LORD delivers him from them all.*
>
> —Psalm 34:19, NIV

God's plan for your life is far bigger than you can imagine, and it requires you to *fear not,* trust Him, and take bold steps. God promised, "I will give you every place where you set your foot" (Joshua 1:3, NIV).

When you follow God wholeheartedly, you can walk confidently into everything He has for you, knowing that He has given you dominion and authority to take the land. With God on your side, you and He are a majority!

YOU WIN: What does it look like for you to follow God wholeheartedly in your current season? Reflect on one area where you can trust Him more fully and take a bold step forward.

DAY 18

VICTORY IS IN MY STEP!

> *Now thanks be to God who always leads us in triumph in Christ, and through us diffuses the fragrance of His knowledge in every place.*
>
> —2 Corinthians 2:14, NKJV

Victory is in your step. "Every place that the sole of your foot will tread upon I have given to you" (Joshua 1:3, NIV). That was the word God gave to Joshua. He basically said to him, "Go and possess the land. You're well able."

When I was just starting in real estate—and honestly, many times since—I took that promise and made it practical. I'm a practical, tactical kind of person. I ask myself, "How do I apply the Bible, make it work in my world, and see the truth play out in today's timeframe?"

So, here's what I did. In real estate, I'd write down all the listings I needed to sell or the buyers I needed to find homes for on a piece of paper. Then, I'd stick that paper in my shoes. I'd write on it: "Every place that the sole of my foot treads upon, I declare it—these listings are sold. Everything is sold in Jesus' name."

And then I'd walk on it. I'd talk about it. Every day, I'd declare it. Sometimes, even at an appointment at a client's house, I'd slip my shoe off and that piece of paper would pop out—it was a little embarrassing, but it worked!

There's something powerful about walking on top of your circumstances. It's a mental and spiritual declaration: "You're under my feet. I've got this in Jesus' name." Whether it's a mountain of debt, an unsold house, a tough situation, or a wayward child, I'd declare victory as I walked.

Victory is in your step. As you walk, talk, and speak on it, you're standing in faith, reminding yourself and the enemy that the battle is already won.

So, here's my challenge: Put it in your shoe. Walk on it until you see the victory! It's just one of the ways I like to win.

The Bible says, "The God of peace will soon crush Satan under your feet" (Romans 16:20a, NLT). See? You win!

YOU WIN: What is a specific situation or challenge you need to declare victory over? Write it down, and then take a physical step—such as walking or even writing it on paper and placing it under your foot—as a declaration of faith that God has already given you the victory.

DAY 19

THE POWER OF YOUR CHOICE

> *But if serving the LORD seems undesirable to you, then choose for yourselves this day whom you will serve, whether the gods your ancestors served beyond the Euphrates, or the gods of the Amorites, in whose land you are living. But as for me and my household, we will serve the LORD.*
>
> —Joshua 24:15, NIV

During a visit with Ruth Ann, I asked her how she was doing. Her response struck me deeply:

> *Every morning when I wake up, I have to choose to be happy. I have to make a decided decision to be happy. I spend most of my days lying in this bed, and if I just let the day go by how I feel in the morning—discouraged, hopeless, and frustrated by my lack of ability to be purposeful—I wouldn't have one good day. So, as soon as my eyes open, I declare, "This is the day the LORD has made; [I] will rejoice and be glad in it" (Psalm 118:24, NKJV).*

I thought to myself, *This is so true for all of us.* It's not physiologically feasible to wake up laughing—we don't have enough oxygen in our brains at that point to feel that way! It's so easy to wake up feeling sad, discouraged, or even overwhelmed.

That's why we have to *choose*. Every single day, in so many scenarios, we must choose to be happy. Our choice to be happy is our power position.

The truth is, you only have control over two things in life: your attitude and your actions. It all comes down to choosing.

- I choose to believe the Word of God.
- I choose to surrender to His plans for my life.
- I choose joy.
- I choose to act in love.
- I choose to forgive.

Make the decision first thing in the morning: "This is the day the LORD has made; we will rejoice and be glad in it" (Psalm 118:24, NKJV). Setting your mind this way draws you into abundance and gratitude. It's like setting your sail toward happiness.

You also have to choose which report you'll believe. Will you believe the report of the Lord (the Bible) or the report of man? Will you listen to the whispers of doubt, lack, or insecurity? Or will you choose what God says about you? God says:

- You are made in His image (Genesis 1:27).
- You are a child of God (John 1:12; Romans 8:15).
- You are well able (Numbers 13:30; Philippians 4:13).

The report you choose will be produced after its kind. If you choose the world's report, you'll reap anxiety, fear, and discouragement. But if you choose to believe God's Word, it will produce strength, joy, and a sense of being "well able" in your mind, will, and emotions.

Choose wisely! You win!

YOU WIN: What choice can you make today to align your attitude and actions with God's promises? Write a declaration for the day.

DAY 20

THE PURPOSE OF PAIN

Consider it pure joy, my brothers and sisters, whenever you face trials of many kinds, because you know that the testing of your faith produces perseverance. Let perseverance finish its work so that you may be mature and complete, not lacking anything.
—James 1:2-4, NIV

I was having a discussion with Ruth Ann, and she made a statement that struck me: "God doesn't let the righteous suffer unless there is a plus in it."

Curious, I asked her to tell me more. She explained that in the biggest trials of her life, those very trials became the doorway to her greatest blessings.

Trials require something of us:

- You have to grow better under trials.
- They will often require you to find a new promise from the Word of God.
- You learn to bet your life on the promises of God.

And we know that in all things God works for the good of those who love him, who have been called according to his purpose.
—Romans 8:28, NIV

All things? Really? In life's most difficult situations, we have to trust that God knows the beginning from the end, even when we only see in part. As human beings, it's hard to stay locked into that perspective.

I don't believe God puts illness or tragedy on our lives, but I do believe that everything passes through His hands. Consider Job—he loved God and was upright, yet he endured intense affliction at the hand of the enemy. God allowed it, knowing Job would pass the test and be restored double.

The pain in our lives often serves the greatest purpose. None of us like the furnace of affliction, yet when you walk through the fire and stay free of bitterness and cynicism, it becomes a point of connection with others. It lays a foundation of faith.

I believe the enemy of our soul has some idea of the impact our lives will have on this earth; the greater the potential impact, the more challenges seem to show up.

Just like muscles are built with resistance, faith muscles are strengthened through trials. The bigger the call, the stronger the faith muscles you'll need.

So, lock in. Decide to fix your eyes on the Author and Perfecter of your faith. This is critical. You must have a fixed, unshakable faith to walk through to victory—even when the storms of difficulty rage or it seems like nothing is changing.

Know this: the God who hung the stars and set the earth in order is working behind the scenes on your behalf. He is arranging things and people for your good.

As Ruth Ann has reminded me so many times, "God meant it for good!"

YOU WIN: Reflect on a trial or painful experience in your life. How might God use it for your growth or as a doorway to blessings? Write a prayer asking Him to help you trust His purpose, even when it's hard to see.

DAY 21

YOU SERVE A WINNING GOD

Then you will make your way prosperous, and then you will have good success.
—Joshua 1:8, NKJV

God always has a way of winning.

The thief comes only to steal and kill and destroy; I came that they may have and enjoy life, and have it in abundance [to the full, till it overflows].
—John 10:10, AMP

And God is able to bless you abundantly, so that in all things at all times, having all that you need, you will abound in every good work.
—2 Corinthians 9:8, NIV

And my God will meet all your needs according to the riches of his glory in Christ Jesus.
—Philippians 4:19, NIV

*The L*ORD *is my shepherd; I lack nothing.*
He makes me lie down in green pastures,
he leads me beside quiet waters,
he refreshes my soul.
He guides me along the right paths for his name's sake.
Even though I walk through the darkest valley,
I will fear no evil, for you are with me;
your rod and your staff, they comfort me.

> *You prepare a table before me in the presence of my enemies.*
> *You anoint my head with oil; my cup overflows.*
> *Surely your goodness and love will follow me all the days of my life,*
> *and I will dwell in the house of the LORD forever.*
> —Psalm 23, NIV

Doesn't that sound like a winning God? When we feel weak and feeble, the Bible reminds us: "My grace is sufficient for you, for my power is made perfect in weakness" (2 Corinthians 12:9, NIV). When we yield and rely on Him, He girds us with strength and makes our way perfect.

> *And we know that in all things God works for the good of those who love him, who have been called according to his purpose.*
> —Romans 8:28, NIV

You can't lose if you don't quit. In your battle, may you echo the psalmist: "I remain confident of this: I will see the goodness of the LORD in the land of the living" (Psalm 27:13, NIV).

Even when you feel like you can't go on, God says, "Open wide your mouth and I will fill it" (Psalm 81:10, NIV). He will give you the words to speak, the wisdom to take the next step, and the power to overcome and win in all things.

"I am the God who fills all in all." Speak to the barren places, the hard spots, and the difficult situations, and ask God to fill them with His fullness. Watch as His supernatural supply shifts every circumstance in your favor.

It might not—and likely will not—happen overnight. "Let patience have her perfect work, that ye may be perfect and entire, lacking nothing" (James 1:4, KJV).

> *If any of you lacks wisdom, you should ask God, who gives generously to all without finding fault, and it will be given to you.*

But when you ask, you must believe and not doubt, because the one who doubts is like a wave of the sea, blown and tossed by the wind.

—James 1:5-6, NIV

You will see the faithfulness of God if you do not faint.

YOU WIN: Are there areas of your life that feel barren or lacking right now? Write a declaration of God's promises over that situation, speaking abundance, provision, and victory.

DAY 22

GOD IS A RESTORER

> *And the LORD restored Job's losses when he prayed for his friends. Indeed the LORD gave Job twice as much as he had before.*
>
> —Job 42:10, NKJV

God is a restorer. Have you ever thought about that? God is a restorer of all things. He restores peace. He restores your soul. I often remind myself that He's the restorer of my soul—my mind, my will, and my emotions. The Bible says, "He restores my soul" (Psalm 23:3, NKJV).

But today, I want to talk to you about the power of your words—specifically, the power of saying, *"Restore."*

Look around your life. Have you ever felt lost? Have you ever felt like something has been stolen from you? Maybe a vacation turned into a disaster. Maybe your relationships feel like they're riding the struggle bus. Perhaps your business, which once thrived, feels unrecognizable now.

The Bible says, "The thief comes only to steal and kill and destroy; I have come that they may have life, and have it to the full" (John 10:10, NIV).

When we think about restoration, so much of it is tied to the words we speak. I've found myself in places of lack, struggle, and loss, where I've simply started to speak the word *restore*. Over and over again, I've spoken "restore, restore, restore" to those areas.

The Bible promises, "If he is caught, he must pay back sevenfold" (Proverbs 6:31, NIV). How much money, how many opportunities, how many years have been lost? Years lost to bitterness, depression, discouragement, or sitting on the sidelines? Yet God says He will redeem the time. He promises, "I will repay you for the years the locusts have eaten" (Joel 2:25, NIV).

Isaiah speaks of people being trapped and having no one to say "restore." But God says, "I say, restore" (Isaiah 42:22, paraphrased). There's so much power in speaking restoration. When you start to declare "restore" over areas of loss or struggle, you'll begin to see things shift.

Speaking "restore" leads you to prayer. In the Bible, Job is an example of restoration. He was wealthy, healthy, and blessed, but in just nine months, he lost everything—his wealth, his health, even his family. Yet, the Bible says, "After Job had prayed for his friends, the LORD restored his fortunes and gave him twice as much as he had before" (Job 42:10, NIV).

Part of restoration is stepping outside of yourself. Think about the friends in your life who need restoration. Take your eyes off your own circumstances and begin speaking restoration over others.

Many mornings on my walk, I'll just start speaking "restore" over people I know who need it. I don't even talk about my own problems—God already knows what I'm facing. Instead, I thank Him for the answers and solutions and keep speaking "restore" over others.

As Job prayed for his friends, the Lord restored him and gave him double for his trouble. *Double for your trouble!* That's restoration.

What do you need to speak "restore" to? Who do you need to pray for? Make a list and take your eyes off yourself. Start speaking the word "restore" over your life and the lives of others.

I also believe God will lead you to sow a seed of restoration—something intentional. Sow it into something thriving and name that seed "restoration." This has been a game-changer for me. But as you do this, examine your heart. Let go of any unforgiveness or discouragement. Then take action.

The Bible says that as you go, step by step, He will open up the way before you (Proverbs 4:12, NIV).

As you speak "restore," God will lead you to take practical steps—make the phone call, send the text, extend grace, or give generously. God is a restorer, and when He restores, He does it abundantly. He doesn't just restore things to their original state—He restores them better. You'll come out transformed.

Here are a few Scriptures that promise restoration:

- "I will repay you for the years the locusts have eaten" (Joel 2:25, NIV).

- "The LORD your God will restore your fortunes and have compassion on you" (Deuteronomy 30:3, NIV).

- "But I will restore you to health and heal your wounds" (Jeremiah 30:17, NIV).

- "After Job had prayed for his friends, the LORD restored his fortunes and gave him twice as much as he had before" (Job 42:10, NIV).

God promises to redeem lost time and bring abundance, even after seasons of hardship.

What do you need to speak "restore" to today? Believe God is a restorer and expect to see His restoring power at work in your life.

YOU WIN: Is there something in your life or someone that you care about that feels lost, broken, or stolen? Write it down, then write "restore" over it. Speak "restore" out loud, asking God to bring restoration and abundance beyond what you've imagined.

DAY 23

SING TO YOURSELF

> *Speaking to yourselves in psalms and hymns and spiritual songs, singing and making melody in your heart to the Lord; Giving thanks always for all things unto God and the Father in the name of our Lord Jesus Christ;*
>
> —Ephesians 5:19-20, KJV

One of the keys to winning is that you have to sing to yourself, speak to yourself, and prophesy over your future.

When we're walking through hard things or difficulties, sometimes we wake up feeling so heavy. Your heart feels weighed down, like you're facing a mountain of impossibilities. Yet, I'm reminded of the promise: "This is the day the Lord has made; [I] will rejoice and be glad in it" (Psalm 118:24, NKJV).

Sometimes, you just have to talk yourself into joy—prophesy yourself into it—because if you get in agreement with the heaviness, the doubt, and the lack, hope vanishes. The living, active Word of God cannot return void, so you have to get in agreement with the Word.

- The Word says I'm blessed (Deuteronomy 28:3).

- The Word says the work of my hands will prosper and increase (Deuteronomy 28:12).

- The Word says He turns all things for my good (Romans 8:28).

- The Word says He is working on my behalf (Philippians 2:13).

Even when it doesn't look like it, you have to get in agreement with the Word because your circumstances will lie to you.

My husband was flying and working on his IFR rating, which qualifies a pilot to fly in the clouds. During the training, they put goggles on him so he could only see the instruments, not the outside view. While flying, he said, "It felt like we were descending, but the instruments showed we were climbing. Everything in my body told me the opposite, but I had to trust the instruments."

Think about that in life. It can look like you're losing, like everything is working against you. But at the end of the day, there's a foundation being built. God is behind the scenes working on your behalf, and you have to trust that it ends well for you.

You need a deep belief that God is working for you, that you and God are a majority. When you hold onto that belief, no matter what comes against you, you will rise. He will show Himself strong on your behalf.

The Bible says, "The LORD is mighty in battle" (Psalm 24:8, NIV). No matter what war you're fighting, He is your Mighty in Battle.

So, find the promise. Get in the Word of God and find the promise. The Bible says, "Do two walk together unless they have agreed to do so?" (Amos 3:3, NIV). Get in agreement with God. Get in agreement with His Word and say what He says.

I say it all the time: Say what the Bible says. Say what God says. I'll take His living, active, revelatory Word over human opinions any day. When you embrace the Word of God and let it become a part of you, it will transform not only your life and circumstances but also the lives of those around you.

Know this: God always has a plan. Your steps are ordered.

YOU WIN: What promise from God's Word do you need to get into agreement with today? Write it down and speak it over yourself, choosing to trust God's truth above your circumstances.

DAY 24

SPENDING TIME IN THE WORD

> *For the word of God is living and powerful, and sharper than any two-edged sword, piercing even to the division of soul and spirit, and of joints and marrow, and is a discerner of the thoughts and intents of the heart.*
>
> —Hebrews 4:12, NKJV

Another key to success is spending time in the Word of God—the transformational, living, active, breathing Word of God. It's the reader of your life. The Word reads you, showing you where your weakness is, strengthening you, and increasing you. You have to immerse yourself in the Word and know it because, in times of stress and crisis, it will come to your aid and illuminate your path.

I'll never forget this. Four years ago, I went to the doctor and received an unwanted health diagnosis. I was stunned—overwhelmed with fear. At the time, I had six-year-old twins, and I told my doctor, "Just remember, I have six-year-old twins. I need to live a long time to raise them."

He said, "Amy, remember when you were selling our home, and I was so concerned and you looked at me and said, 'Let me worry about those details. I got you!' Well now, I've got you!" Those words were so comforting. But while he was talking, I kept hearing a Scripture that I hadn't thought about in a long time: "When you pass through the waters, they'll not overwhelm you. When you walk through the fire, you won't be burned."

That verse was so loud, so strong—it felt louder than the doctor's words.

> *When you pass through the waters, I will be with you; and when you pass through the rivers, they will not sweep over you. When you walk through the fire, you will not be burned; the flames will not set you ablaze.*
>
> —Isaiah 43:2, NIV

That Word became my lifeline. No matter what anyone else said during my healing journey, I clung to it. It was living, active, and illuminated to me—it was God speaking directly through His Word.

I had hidden that Scripture in my heart long ago without even realizing it. It was something I had read over the years, and in that moment, it became a profound source of comfort and hope. It was my key: *I'm going to win!*

I repeated Isaiah 43:2 every time fear or overwhelm tried to consume me: "When you pass through the waters, they will not overwhelm you. When you walk through the fire, you will not be burned" (NIV).

When we hide the Word in our hearts, it becomes a wellspring in times of crisis. The Bible says, "Yea though I walk through the valley of the shadow of death, I will fear no evil; For You are with me" (Psalm 23:4, NKJV). We will walk through valleys—it's part of life. No one is exempt from crisis or trouble.

But being a follower of Jesus gives us the grace and ability to move through it. He doesn't stop the valleys from coming, but He sustains you through them, transforms you through them, and brings you to a better place on the other side. If you hold closely to Him, He will illuminate your path and lead you to victory.

So, get the Word in your heart. Hide it there for the "rainy day" when you'll need it. When that Word rises up in your spirit during a crisis, it blasts through the darkness, the lack, the diagnosis—it becomes a bright light in the shadows.

The Word sustained me through many scary days, countless doctor's appointments, and every step of the healing process.

Think about a time when you faced a challenge and a Bible verse you hadn't read or thought about in years rose in your spirit. It's a powerful moment when you realize the God of the universe cares so deeply for you that He illuminates His promises at just the right time.

Feed your spirit with the Word of God. It will transform you, sustain you, and keep you. It will comfort you in the night and lead you to victory.

YOU WIN: Do you have a time when a Bible verse (or a quote) that God used to encourage you during a challenge? Write it down, then ask God to highlight a new verse to you.

DAY 25

THE PRISION OF INCONSISTENCY

Jesus Christ is the same yesterday, today, and forever.
—Hebrews 13:8, NKJV

Inconsistency—everyone deals with it. Did you know that approximately 92% of people who set New Year's resolutions or goals have completely given up on them by February 1st? Ninety-two percent! That's an astounding statistic.

This means most people are not moving forward into a future that's any different from the one they're already living in.

The truth is, inconsistency is the enemy of your future. It's a well-laid strategy of the enemy to keep you small and wandering in the wilderness of your own life.

We're made in the likeness of God, right? And God is consistent. The sun rises and sets every single day. He created consistency. The Bible says, "Jesus Christ is the same yesterday and today and forever" (Hebrews 13:8, NIV).

I believe inconsistency is the lever the enemy uses to keep you stuck, to keep you from becoming all you're meant to be. Inconsistency holds you back from fully stepping into your God-given purpose. Think about it—the enemy doesn't come after your dreams directly. Instead, he attacks you with inconsistency.

It's subtle but massive.

What does it look like? It shows up in the small, everyday things. For example, at night, I get so excited about my plans. I'll set my alarm for 4:45 AM, fired up to crush my goals in the morning. Then 4:45 rolls around, and guess what? I think, "Hit snooze."

My mind starts to counsel me: "This is crazy. Your body needs rest. No one's going to know if you skip today. Start tomorrow."

When I listen to those thoughts and take that counsel, I've just done something significant: I've disappointed myself.

And here's why that matters—your voice is the most influential voice in your world. Not staying true to your micro-commitments doesn't just make you feel bad about yourself; it also creates a cycle of negative self-talk.

Inconsistency whispers, "It's fine. Just skip today." But skipping today becomes skipping tomorrow, and before you know it, you're stuck, frustrated, and stagnant.

Inconsistency isn't just a habit—it's a prison. But the good news is, you hold the key.

Start small. Follow through on those micro-commitments. Break free from the cycle of inconsistency and step into the life you're meant to live!

The inconsistent life will always be limited in its influence and impact. How do we overcome the trap of inconsistency? Here are a few practical steps:

1. **Write the vision.** Sit down and make it clear. Look at it every day because a fuzzy future doesn't have much pull power.

2. **Get back on the horse.** If you've fallen into inconsistency (and let's be honest, most of us have), just start again.

3. **Recognize your excuses.** Be aware of thought patterns that keep you stuck. Turn the key with consistent activity and unlock your future. Your excuses are like bars in a prison cell. They sound reasonable:

   - "I need to wait for God's timing."

   - "I'll pray about it some more."

   - "Now isn't the right season."

4. **Start small with micro-commitments.** Overwhelmed? Break it down. Can't join the 5 a.m. club? Just wake up 15 minutes earlier. If you're a night owl, work when you're at your best—but stay consistent.

5. **Celebrate your wins.** Track your victories, no matter how small. Write them down and remind yourself: "I won today. I had a consistent week. I'm building something great."

When you lock into your vision and truly commit, consistency becomes easier. Why? Because something inside of you compels you.

If you keep seeing something in your mind—a dream, a goal—that's your preview of the future God has for you. But to make it real, you need consistent, daily action.

This isn't just about you. Your family is counting on you. Your future is counting on you. This generation is counting on you to be all that you're created to be.

Society's gravitational pull is to lull you into average. It glorifies comfort, but comfort is your enemy. Everyone I know in the Bible faced their own battles with consistency. They fought to become who God called them to be.

Inconsistency is a worthy foe, but if you master it, you will walk among the greats.

You were made to win!

YOU WIN: What small, consistent action can you take today to break free from inconsistency? Write down one micro-commitment you will stick to this week and how you'll celebrate when you succeed.

DAY 26

GRACE, GRACE

> *"Who are you, O great mountain? Before Zerubbabel you shall become a plain! And he shall bring forth the capstone With shouts of 'Grace, grace to it!'"*
>
> —Zachariah 4:7, NKJV

When I read Zechariah 4:7 several years ago, it became a revelation for me. The Amplified version says: "What are you, O great mountain [of human obstacles]? Before Zerubbabel you shall become a plain [insignificant]! And he will bring out the capstone with loud shouts of 'Grace, grace to it'" (AMP).

Grace, as defined by Webster, is "a simple elegance or refinement of movement." I think of grace like oil that makes everything move smoothly—a balm for hard situations.

I've made it a practice to speak grace into situations. It's become one of my go-to tools, and I've seen its transformative, mountain-moving power in so many areas of my life.

I speak grace on the way to making difficult phone calls, navigating seemingly impossible real estate transactions, and preparing for important conversations with some of the most meaningful people in my life. Grace has the power to bring resolution, shift mindsets, and provide supernatural aid to make the crooked, treacherous places in life straight.

When you face a mountain of human obstacles, I encourage you to literally say, "I speak grace, grace, grace to this situation." Watch how it brings ease and transformation as you develop this practice into a lifestyle.

This revelation has been a winning strategy for me for decades. When I don't know what to do, I shout *"Grace!"*

My sister even painted a wall hanging for me that says, "Grace, Grace, Grace." I look at it every day with gratitude, knowing that I walk in the unmerited, unearned grace of God.

Grace has the power to destroy walls of resistance and dissolve obstacles that seem to have no answers. When applied to challenging situations, it can bring wisdom, create access points for conversations, and provide solutions to problems.

Give it a try. Speak grace over your life today, and remember…you win!

YOU WIN: Is there a mountain or obstacle are you facing right now? Write it down, then write "Grace, grace!" over that situation. Declare it out loud, trusting God to make the crooked paths straight.

DAY 27

THE GET-BACK-UP LIFE

For though the righteous fall seven times, they rise again, but the wicked stumble when calamity strikes.
—Proverbs 24:16, NIV

*Do not gloat over me, my enemy! Though I have fallen, I will rise. Though I sit in darkness, the L*ORD *will be my light.*
—Micah 7:8, NIV

I was sitting on a plane recently, talking about life, business, and health with my friend Marti. She looked at me and said, "Amy, the only hit that counts is the one you don't get up from."

I paused and said, "Heck yes!"

God has given us the ability to keep getting back up. When Jesus rose from the dead with resurrection power, it wasn't just His victory—it means we can rise again too. If He got back up and was victorious, we can get back up and be victorious as well.

I often tell my team that I've had more "at-bats" than most—and I've failed more than most too. But here's the difference: I didn't quit. Even when I desperately wanted to, I didn't stop.

Like many of you, I've felt the sting of rejection, the torment of self-doubt, and the grip of comparison. I've battled condemnation at times in my life. We all have.

So how do you keep going through the dark times or after significant blows?

For me, it's often because I have others depending on me and quitting simply isn't an option. At my lowest points, I've heard the quiet whisper of God in my heart saying, *"Get up. Get up."*

And so, I would.

I'd commit to doing the next right thing. I'd find someone in a more difficult situation and help them. I'd look for someone whose business was struggling more than mine and lend a hand. I'd reach out to someone facing health challenges or strained relationships and encourage them. Maybe I'd send flowers, a gift card, a meal, or just make a phone call. You don't have to look far to find someone in need.

What I've discovered is this: when I take those steps outside of myself, it not only blesses and encourages others, but it also starts to shift something inside of me. My "mojo" returns, my energy lifts, and I find my strength increasing.

> *A generous person will prosper; whoever refreshes others will be refreshed.*
>
> —Proverbs 11:25, NIV

Nelson Mandela once said, "Our greatest glory is not in never falling, but in rising every time we fall."

So, pop back up and begin again. God is with you, cheering you on, and leading you toward brighter days. "Although your former state was ordinary, your future will be extraordinary (Job 8:7, CEB).

YOU WIN: Think about a time when you faced a setback or failure but got back up. What helped you rise again, and how can you apply that same perseverance to a challenge you're currently facing?

DAY 28

REVIVING DRY BONES

The hand of the LORD was on me, and he brought me out by the Spirit of the LORD and set me in the middle of a valley; it was full of bones. He led me back and forth among them, and I saw a great many bones on the floor of the valley, bones that were very dry. He asked me, "Son of man, can these bones live?"

I said, "Sovereign LORD , you alone know."

Then he said to me, "Prophesy to these bones and say to them, 'Dry bones, hear the word of the LORD! This is what the Sovereign LORD says to these bones: I will make breath enter you, and you will come to life. I will attach tendons to you and make flesh come upon you and cover you with skin; I will put breath in you, and you will come to life. Then you will know that I am the LORD.'"

So I prophesied as I was commanded. And as I was prophesying, there was a noise, a rattling sound, and the bones came together, bone to bone. I looked, and tendons and flesh appeared on them and skin covered them, but there was no breath in them.

Then he said to me, "Prophesy to the breath; prophesy, son of man, and say to it, 'This is what the Sovereign LORD says: Come, breath, from the four winds and breathe into these slain, that they may live.'"

> *So I prophesied as he commanded me, and breath entered them; they came to life and stood up on their feet—a vast army.*
>
> —Ezekiel 37:1-10, NIV

Are you aware that you can be the prophet over your own life?

When I first read the Scripture that says God "calls those things which do not exist as though they did" (Romans 4:17, NKJV), it hit me. I realized I had the ability to speak life and declare things into existence in my own life.

At the time, I had a thriving career and a wonderful family, but I was single with no real prospects of marriage. I looked around, and there was no one in my community who interested me. It felt barren, and at times, hopeless, to think I'd find my person in the small market I lived in (this was before online dating became popular).

One day, while driving down the road, I decided to call forth the spouse that God had for me. I began to speak life over that area and declare that the God who "fills all in all" (Ephesians 1:23, NKJV) would breathe life into my situation.

It didn't happen overnight, but within a few weeks, I began to feel hope arise. And hope—it's the magnet that activates our faith to produce the outcomes we're believing for.

About six months later, my now-husband, Steve, came into my life. God is so faithful. What had once been barren, frustrating, and lonely became a place of joy and fulfillment.

I believe your *voice-activated faith* can shift the narrative of your life. What do you need to speak life into today?

- A dead marriage?
- An unfulfilling career?

- A struggling bank account?
- Your health?
- Infertility?

Be the prophet over your own life. As you consistently speak life and prophesy over the areas that concern you, you will see the hand of God at work. "The LORD will perfect that which concerns me" (Psalm 138:8, NKJV).

YOU WIN: Write a declaration of life and restoration over any situation in your life or the life of a loved one, then speak God's promises with boldness out loud.

DAY 29

GIVE THANKS ALWAYS

> *Rejoice always, pray continually, give thanks in all circumstances; for this is God's will for you in Christ Jesus.*
> —1 Thessalonians 5:16-18, NIV

A strong key to a life that wins is an attitude of gratitude. Gratitude is the ultimate state of receiving. God commands to give thanks in all things!

I've noticed that the more successful an individual is, the more I see extreme gratitude as a foundational part of their life. You might think, *"Well, of course—they're successful, so they have reasons to be grateful."*

But if you dig into most people's stories, you'll find that they've faced countless challenges and adversities. They've had reasons to quit and not get back up. What sustained them—and continues to sustain them—is their gratitude.

It's gratitude at its most basic level: gratitude for waking up in the morning, for having breath in their lungs, for the opportunity to start fresh or serve another person. Gratitude for being able to see, hear, walk—simple, yet profound thankfulness for life itself.

When you spend time each morning in gratitude and thankfulness, it shifts the atmosphere of your mind and emotions. Gratitude positions you to receive even more things to be grateful for.

Your mind is like a magnet, drawing evidence of what you focus on into your life. That's why the Bible says, "For as he thinks in his heart, so is he" (Proverbs 23:7, NKJV).

You are the captain of your own ship. What you think about, you ruminate on—and what you ruminate on, you bring into your life. Life will give you exactly what you expect from it.

Here's the key: when you change how you look at things, the things you look at change.

We all know people who see the glass as half-empty, no matter how blessed they are. You could hand them everything, and it still wouldn't feel like enough. Then there are those who are deeply grateful for even the smallest acts of kindness or generosity.

Who do you want to pour into more—the grateful or the ungrateful? Exactly! Gratitude is magnetic.

When you choose to live with thankfulness, people respond to you differently. It's not about denying the existence of hard and difficult things in life—life is hard by its very nature. But when you intentionally focus on what you have to be thankful for, you create an atmosphere of positivity that draws people to you.

Gratitude helps you see possibilities where others only see obstacles. It gives you strength to rise when you feel like you can't take the next step. It brings light into the darkness.

Gratitude is the key to winning in life.

YOU WIN: List at least three things you're grateful for today—big or small. How does focusing on gratitude shift your perspective?

DAY 30

PRAY BOLD PRAYERS

> *Now to Him who is able to [carry out His purpose and] do superabundantly more than all that we dare ask or think [infinitely beyond our greatest prayers, hopes, or dreams], according to His power that is at work within us…*
> —Ephesians 3:20, AMP

You serve a big God!

I don't know about you, but I can hardly wrap my mind around what "infinitely beyond" means. Our belief systems and minds tend to place such limitations on God. We confine Him with the ceiling of our own doubts and restrictions. But the Bible tells us to ask largely.

Terri Savelle Foy shares a story about praying and hearing God say, "Ask Me to do something that makes Me look like God."

Yet so often, we shrink our prayers down to, "Lord, if I could just…"

- If I could just find a job…
- If I could just find a spouse…
- If I could just…

We're praying too small. It's time to get bold in our prayers and ask for BIG, SPECIFIC things. Things so big that only God can accomplish them. Things that require us to stretch our faith and believe God for the impossible.

The Bible says, "With God, nothing will be impossible" (Luke 1:37, NKJV). You might think, "I know nothing is impossible for God—but will He do it for me?"

If you have the faith to believe that He can and will, He will. Faith is a muscle that grows with use. The Bible says, "So then faith comes by hearing, and hearing by the word of God" (Romans 10:17, NKJV).

Can you really increase your faith? Absolutely, yes!

- Read the Word of God.
- Listen to preaching, messages, and testimonies of others.

You must choose to exercise and grow your spirit man—your faith center. Feed it the right things. When you feed on God's Word, your faith is strengthened and increased. The Word creates vision in your heart and life.

Know that God is a God of increase: "May the LORD give you increase more and more, you and your children" (Psalm 115:14-15, NKJV).

If you're in a season where you feel diminished, know this: God may allow it for a time, but it doesn't have to define your future. Often, He is refining and redirecting you during those seasons. And when you come out, you will be stronger, more able, and more impactful!

God backs you. He always wants to increase you. With God on your side, you can't lose. You and God are a majority!

Pray largely. Ask big.

A great starting point is the prayer of Jabez. Jabez is mentioned only briefly in the Bible, but his story is profound. His mother named him Jabez, meaning pain or sorrow, marking him with that identity. Yet Jabez knew God had a different plan for him.

This is Jabez's prayer:

And Jabez called on the God of Israel saying, "Oh, that You would bless me indeed, and enlarge my territory, that Your hand would be with me, and that You would keep me from evil, that I may not cause pain!" So God granted him what he requested.
—1 Chronicles 4:10, NKJV

- Bless me indeed: God's blessing is an empowerment to increase. When God blesses something, it grows and expands.

- Enlarge my territory: Ask for influence and the ability to impact more lives with God's goodness.

- Let Your hand be with me: Never move without God's presence. With Him, you have everything; without Him, you have nothing.

- Keep me from harm: Pray for protection from the pitfalls that could derail your future—wrong relationships, jobs, or decisions.

The key to walking in the ever-increasing plans of God is to continue speaking what He says about you. As you feed your spirit with faith-affirming words, messages, and songs, you will step boldly into all that you were created to do and be.

Heaven responds to bold requests. Ask largely. Believe for big things.

YOU WIN: What big, bold prayer can you bring to God today? Write it out, be specific, and believe that He is able to do infinitely more than you can ask or imagine.

_____

_____

_____

CONCLUSION

I hope you have found this devotional to be transformational to the way you think and live. My prayer is that this book becomes a resource you can jump into at any time, finding encouragement exactly when you need it. As I wrote this devotional, my prayer was that you would see God in a new light—a God who is for you, who desires your good success.

The Bible says, "This Book of the Law shall not depart from your mouth, but you shall meditate in it day and night, that you may observe to do according to all that is written in it. For then you will make your way prosperous, and then you will have good success" (Joshua 1:8, NKJV).

The words written in Scripture are alive to me. They are truths that have sustained me in seasons of adversity and in times of great growth. These Scriptures and the truths within them—when applied—have the power to transform even the most difficult situations.

My prayer for you is twofold:

- "May he give you the desire of your heart and make all your plans succeed" (Psalm 20:4, NIV).
- "The LORD will guide you always; he will satisfy your needs in a sun-scorched land and will strengthen your frame. You will be like a well-watered garden, like a spring whose waters never fail" (Isaiah 58:11, NIV).

May the transformative power of the Word take hold of your life and your heart.

And as Ruth Ann always says to me, "If you have God on your side—you can't lose!"

And that's why you win!

AMY WIENANDS

Wife, mother to twins, and President/CEO of Amy Wienands Real Estate.

For nearly three decades, Amy has been committed to creating an impact in her community and the growth of those around her, through the vehicle of real estate.

After 20 years as an independent agent, Amy took a leap of faith and started the Cedar Valley's first team-centric real estate office—Amy Wienands Real Estate.

Amy and her team have been consistently ranked as one of the Top 100 Teams in the Nation, and Iowa's #1 team of REALTORS® for the past 8 years. Starting with a staff of just two in 2013, the team sits at more than 30 and continues to grow. Purpose and a servant's heart led her team to embody their slogan, "Obsessively Working for You."

It's not all real estate for Amy, though. Her biggest passion in this life is to help people live out their purpose. She knows she's been put on this earth for "more" and is called to inspire, motivate, and leave a significant mark on this world.

She is the host of the *You Are More* podcast, a place of revelation and encouragement for all, and a pillar of faith for many. Amy is a firm believer that hard work, principles of faith, and having the "pop-back" factor are the keys to success.

For more information, visit YOUAREMORE.COM.

YOU ARE MORE PODCAST

There's always been something on the inside of me that continues to whisper that I was created for something more, and that we are all put on this earth for a greater purpose.

You Are More embodies the intention to bring inspiration, revelation, and encouragement for all. I hope to inspire people to walk in the journey and purpose (your supreme reason for being) they were created for.

Through the principles and topics in this podcast, look for direction and guidance to encourage you and inspire you to become all that you are destined for.

Let your dreams and desires be released, and let your heart shift to hopeful expectancy, because YOU ARE MORE!

Check out the *You Are More Podcast* available on Apple podcasts and Spotify, or visit YOUAREMORE.COM.

www.ingramcontent.com/pod-product-compliance
Lightning Source LLC
Chambersburg PA
CBHW071230090426
42736CB00014B/3031